Lucky

The True story of a Duck who thinks that he is a Dog

by Crystal Stockwell

Illustrations by Brian Rice

AuthorHouse™ LLC
1663 Liberty Drive
Bloomington, IN 47403
www.authorhouse.com
Phone: 1-800-839-8640

Published by AuthorHouse 09/16/2013

ISBN: 978-1-4918-1753-7 (sc)
978-1-4918-1754-4 (e)

Library of Congress Control Number: 2013916881

author HOUSE®

There is a little girl named Maya who loves animals.
One day, Maya's dad brought home four ducklings.
Maya named one of the ducklings Lucky.

When Lucky and the other baby ducks were small, they stayed in a cage under a heating lamp in the kitchen. When they started to get their feathers, Maya and her parents would put them in the bathtub and let them splash around.

Lucky and his friends enjoyed this so much, that
when Maya and her parents would open their cage,
the baby ducks would come out by themselves and
run into the bathroom. They would stand by the tub,
and wait to be put into the water.

When Lucky and the other ducks got bigger, Maya's dad put them outside to play in the yard and swim in the pond.

Lucky quickly became friends with Maya's dogs Dodge and Gypsy. Lucky started following the dogs around and acting like them.

Lucky especially became close friends with Gypsy. Lucky enjoys taking walks with Gypsy around the yard and napping with her in the sunshine. Playing chase is one of their favorite games to play together.

If Maya is in the house and Gypsy and Lucky want to get her attention, Gypsy barks for her and Lucky quacks and sometimes even taps on the sliding glass door with his bill.

In the summertime, Lucky, Dodge and Gypsy love to lay in the green grass together while Maya reads stories to them. In the wintertime, Lucky enjoys playing in the snow with Maya and the dogs.

When Maya, her mom or dad come home, Dodge, Gypsy and Lucky all come running to greet them. Lucky loves it when they pick him up and pet him.

At bedtime, the dogs sleep in their dog beds in the garage and Lucky sleeps in the coop with the other ducks. Sometimes, Lucky climbs into one of the dog beds because he would rather sleep there with his friends instead.

If a stranger or another animal comes near the house, the dogs bark and Lucky quacks.

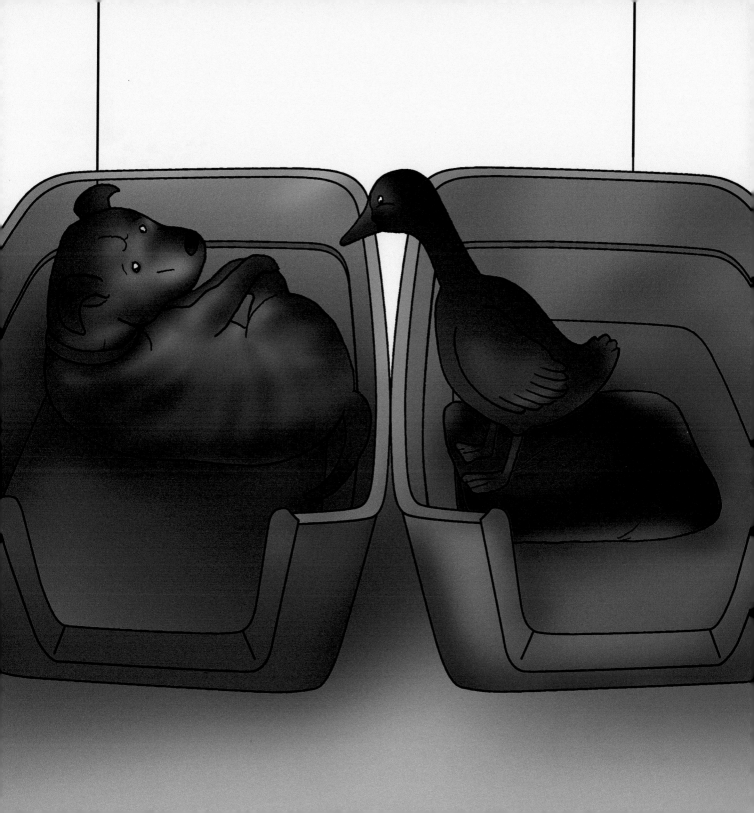

Although Lucky thinks that he is a dog and would rather spend time with Gypsy than the other ducks, he still enjoys swimming in the pond. Sometimes Gypsy even swims with him.

One night when it was time to put the animals to bed, Maya could not find Lucky. Maya and her mom looked everywhere, but no Lucky. Maya went to bed very sad, thinking that Lucky was gone. When Maya's mom woke up in the morning she looked outside and there was Lucky, standing by the pond. She was so happy to see Lucky, that she ran outside in her pajamas and picked him up and hugged him.

Maya was so relieved that her friend was safe. Lucky is a very special duck and a good friend to Dodge, Gypsy, and Maya.

Printed in the United States
by Baker & Taylor Publisher Services